Colors Are Fun, You Will See-

Come Learn The Colors

With Molly And Me!!

**Written and Illustrated
By Candy Johansen**

Thank You Page

I would like to thank my mom, who spoils me and takes extreme good care of me. She spent hours and hours planning, designing and photographing me for this book. I would also like to thank those people who encourage and support mom and I throughout this project.

Miss Molly Mia

Dedication Page

Molly and I would like to dedicate this color
book to my oldest son, Logan. Although Logan
never got to meet Molly, I know he would've
loved and teased her endlessly. Logan colored
our world while he was here with us with
his non-stop talking, laughing and his love
for life. Our world is a little less colorful
without him.

Candy

RED

The color red is used on fire engines to make them stand out. I would make a good fire dog, don't you think? I hid 3 red objects on the fire truck. Can you spot them?

There are lots of
different shades of
Red.
Here are a few of
the shades of Red
we see most often.

I eat apples everyday.
Do you like apples?
I like the apple Red
color. Which apple
would you choose?

Scarlet
Red

Apple
Red

Crimson
Red

Blush
Red

Wine
Red

This is my Red page.
These are some of the
Red items mom and
I found in our house.

Look around your house.
What do you see that is Red?
Do you have any Red toys?
Do you like tomatoes, peppers
strawberries or
apples?

Frisbee

Crayons

Tomato

Apples

Pepper

Shovel

Skittles

Strawberries

M&M's

Red is the international color for stop.

In other cultures, Red has different meanings. In some cultures, red represents purity, joy and celebration and is a traditional color worn by brides. In China, Red is used for good luck and represents happiness and prosperity. In South Africa, Red is the color people wear when they are sad. In the US, red, when combined with white and blue, represent patriotism and pride of country.

Red is energizing. It is often used to express love. It's the color of love, violence, danger, anger and adventure.

Red captures attention. It is a strong color. Red is a very visible color.

Red is the most popular color used on flags in the world.

Red is one of the top two favorite colors of all people.

Do you know why fire hydrants are painted different colors? Fire hydrants are painted different colors to let firefighters know how much water a hydrant will provide.

BLUE

Blue is the all-time favorite color of all people.

Water and the sky are both a blue color.

Can you find 3 more blue items in this photo?

Navy Blue

Azure

Cyan

Powder Blue

Baby Blue

Royal Blue

Carolina Blue

There are lots of different shades of Blue. Here are a few of the shades of Blue we see most often.

My favorite anchor is the Royal Blue one. Which anchor would you choose?

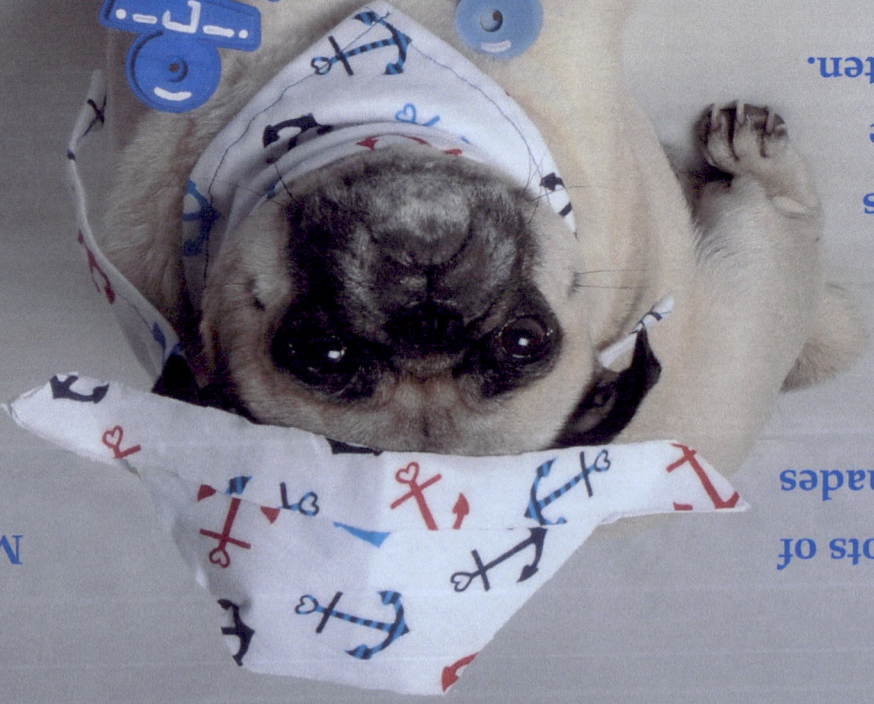

This is my Blue page. I have lots of Blue things. Do you have any favorite Blue toys??

Blue stuffed squeaky toy

My mom made me these Blue pajamas. Do you wear Blue jeans?
I bet you do!!

Blue Bat

Blue Ball

Blue Shovel

Blue Toy

Blue Duck

Blue Crayons

Blue M&M's

Blueberries

Blue Bone Chew Toy

The color Blue is nature's color because water and the sky is Blue.

The color Blue stands for significance, importance, and confidence; that's why police officers and firefighters wear Blue.

Blue is the favorite color of all people.

Most people wear the color Blue everyday. Do you have a pair of Blue jeans?

The color Blue reduces stress and makes us feel calm.

In many cultures, Blue is believed to promote peace. In some countries, people wear Blue when they are sad, but in the United States, Blue is a happy color.

YELLOW

Bright Yellow is the most highly visible of all the colors.

School buses are painted yellow because we can see them easily.

I hid 3 other yellow objects on this page.

Can you find them?

There are lots of different shades of Yellow. Here are a few of the shades of Yellow we see most often.

I like the Banana Yellow flower. Which flower would you pick to give to your mom?

Banana Yellow

Dandelion Yellow

Canary Yellow

Lemon Yellow

Daffodil Yellow

Yellow Ducks

Banana

Yellow Skittles

Yellow M&M's

Yellow Crayons

Yellow Shovel

Lemon

Yellow Pepper

Yellow Flowers

Do you ever pick flowers and give them to someone to make their day better? Try it! Pick a flower and give it to someone and I'll bet you get a smile!!

This is my Yellow page. I like the color Yellow. What is your favorite color?

Yellow is the most highly visible
of all the colors and that is why it is
used for pedestrian crossings,
traffic lights and signs warning
us to be cautious.

Yellow is the color of happiness and
optimism, of sunshine and spring.
The color Yellow stands for
sunshine and warmth.

Yellow helps us focus, study and
remember information.

In different cultures,
Yellow has different meanings.
In some cultures, Yellow
means peace. In Japan,
Yellow stands for courage.
In India, Yellow is the
color of the merchants.

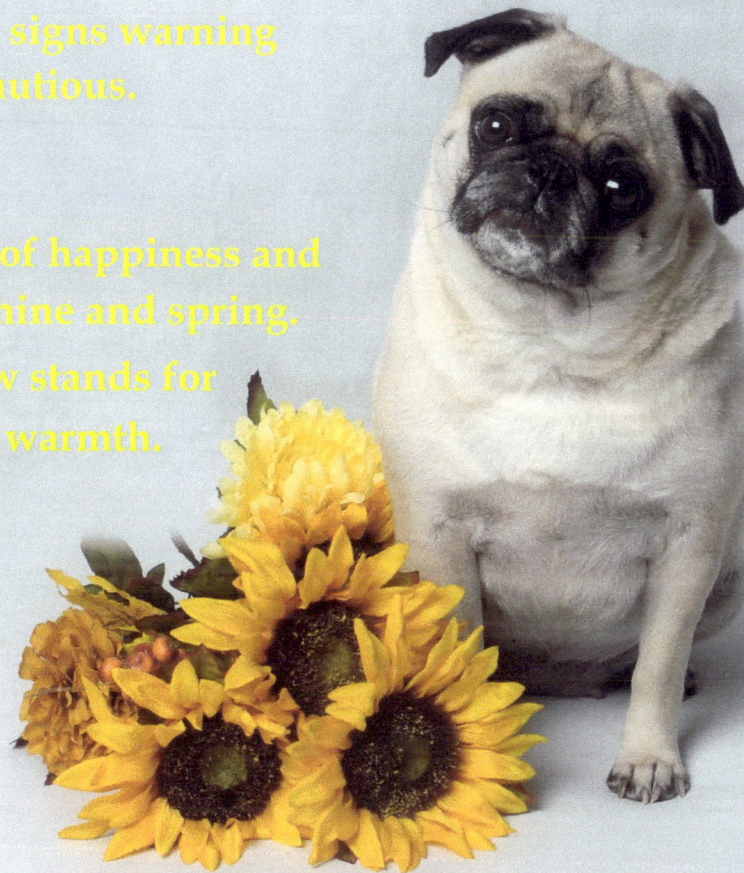

GREEN

I found a green tractor. It was fun to play on.

The color green is the color we see the most around us everday.

I hid 3 green objects on this page.

Do you see them?

There are lots of
different shades of
Green.
Here are a few of
the shades of
Green we see most
often.

I like to go on bike rides
with my mom. I like
the Lime Green bike.
Which bike
would you choose
to ride?

Chartreuse Green

Sage Green

Pine Green

Lime Green

Basil Green

Here is my Green page. These are a few of the Green things I could think of. What do you have that is the color Green?

St. Patrick's Day Hat

Green stuffed snake

My favorite toy is the Green treat toy. I get treats out of it when I roll it around. What color is your favorite toy?

Cabbage

Broccoli

Ball

Pear

Green Skittles

Green M&M's

Green Apple

Green Pepper

Green dog treat toy

When we think of the color Green, we think of growth, nature, harmony, life, renewal, energy, safety, environment, money and finances.

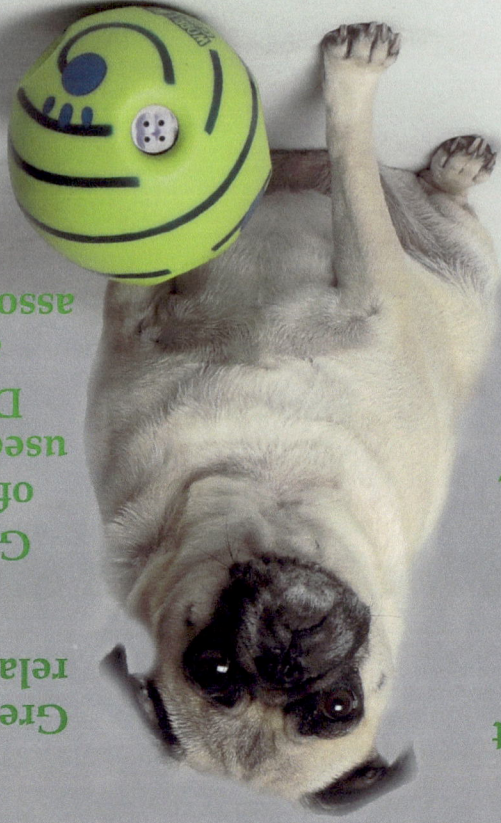

Green is one of the most dominant colors in our world (grass, trees)

Green was the favorite color of George Washington, the first president of the United States.

Green is the national color of Ireland and is the color used to celebrate Saint Patrick's Day. Leprechauns, clovers and good luck are also associated with the color Green.

Green is the most restful and relaxing color for us to look at.

People who love nature, their pets, their homes and like to garden usually like the color Green.

ORANGE

AND

PURPLE

Carrot Orange

Marigold Orange

Cantaloupe Orange

Sandstone Orange

Tangerine Orange

There are many different shades of Orange. Here are a few of the shades of Orange we see most often.

If we were going to play basketball, which Orange ball would you chooose? I want to play with the carrot Orange basketball.

This is my Orange page. Orange is a bright color, isn't it? Can you think of anything you have that is Orange, like maybe an Orange shirt?

Have you ever seen these Orange cones when driving in the car with your mom? These cones warn your mom to be careful when driving because construction workers are working in that area.

Orange Hazard Cone

Orange Hazard Cone

Orange leaves

Orange

Carrots

Ball

Orange M&M's

Orange crayons

Orange skittles

Apricot

My boy's hunting hat

Children love the color orange.

The color Orange is very
visible and is often used
to get attention.
It's the color of life rafts,
hazard cones and high
visibility police vests.

The color Orange is named
after the orange fruit.

Orange is a common color
of citrus fruits and is the
color of vitamin C.

The color Orange is often
thought about as both a
summer color and a fall
color: summer because
of the hot sun and fall
because of pumpkins and
orange leaves.

There are lots of different shades of Purple.
Here are a few of the shades of Purple we see most often.

If I were king for a day, I would choose to wear the Plum Purple crown. If you got to be king, which Purple crown would you want to wear?

Velvet Purple

Mauve

Plum Purple

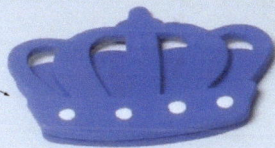

Orchid Purple

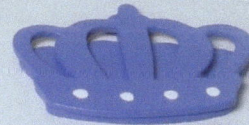

Heather Purple

This is my Purple page.
I like the color Purple
because it's a fun color.
Do you have anything
that is Purple?

I love to sleep on soft pillows.
Do you have a favorite pillow
that you sleep with at night?

Purple
stuffed
toy

Purple
dog
toy

Purple
Skittles

Crayons

Purple
Balls

Purple
stuffed
pillow

Most children love the color Purple and Purple is a favorite color of artists.

Lavender, orchid, lilac and violet flowers are all Purple and considered delicate and precious because the color Purple is not seen very much in nature.

The color Purple is most associated with royalty, magic, and mystery.

In Thailand, Purple is worn when someone is sad. In Japan, the color Purple stands for position and wealth.

In the military, soldiers who are wounded in battle trying to protect their country are awarded a Purple heart award. The award represents courage.

PINK

AND

BROWN

There are lots of different shades of Pink.
Here are a few of the shades of Pink we see most often.

I love my mom and my boy. They've taken good care of me. Who do you love? Who takes good care of you? You should color them a heart. I like the Taffy Pink heart. What color will your heart be?

Blush Pink

Bubblegum Pink

Taffy Pink

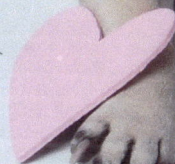

Hot Pink

Magenta Pink

This is my Pink page. These are some of my favorite Pink items. What do you have that is Pink?

Pink Summer Hat

Pink Flower

Pink Bandana

Pink Bunny

Pink Duck

Pink Cowboy Hat

Pink Bear

Pink Ball

Tiny Polka Dot Pink Bear

Pink Crayons

The color Pink usually stands
for compassion, nurturing
(to support or encourage)
and love.

Pink is nornally thought of as
a feminine color (a girl color),
but it's also used for romance,
and affection.

The color Pink calms and
reassures.

Pink is a sign of
unconditional love.

The color Pink stands for
the sweetness and
innocence of a child.

Pink stands for a sign of hope-
a sign that everything will be OK.

This is my Brown page. Do you have a Brown shirt? My mom made me these Brown flannel pajamas. They're really warm.

Do you have any favorite stuffed animals? These are some of my favorite animals. I sleep and snuggle with them.

Brown Lion

Brown Cow

Furry Brown Bear

Brown pug, just like me!!

My favorite stuffed bunny

Brown Crayons

Tiny Brown Bear

Peanuts

The color Brown stands for reliability, security, healing, home, stability, warmth, and honesty.

Brown is the color of the earth, dirt, and wood. Brown is typically associated with the fall and winter seasons.

Brown is the color of the earth, and is a comforting, relaxing color.

When shades of Brown are combined with green, the two colors are used to stand for recycling or earth- friendly.

BLACK
GREY
AND
WHITE

This is my Black page
Let me introduce my sister,
Dolly. Dolly and I are both
pugs, but she's Black and
I am a fawn color.
Dolly's a pretty cool
sister!!

Do you have anything that is
Black? A shirt maybe?? Or a
pair of tennis shoes?

Black
Sunglasses

Black
Pug

Black Hat

Black golf
ball

Black
Crayon

Black dog
Toy

Black
Orca
Whale

In some countries, Black is worn to show that a person is mourning (or sad), like when a person we love, has died.

Lots of times, in television movies, or in books, the person playing the bad guy will wear black and the good guy will wear white.

The color Black can stand for strength, seriousness, power, fear and death.
People wear the color Black in the professional world (lawyers, judges, bankers,) and Black is also worn at formal events (like weddings, funerals, and business meetings.)

Black is known as a mysterious color and is often connected with the unknown or the negative.

Black is the absence of color.

The color Black can make things look smaller, like a bedroom, if painted Black.

This is my Grey page. Can you think of anything you have that is the color Grey?

This stuffed bunny is one of my favorite toys and the Grey leash is what my mom uses to take me for a walk everyday. Do you have a dog that you take for a walk?

Grey stuffed bunny

Grey dog leash

Grey stuffed whale

Grey football

Grey crayons

There are lots of different shades of Brown. Here are a few of the shades of Brown we see most often.

Have you ever seen a deer? Does anyone in your family hunt deer? Which deer looks like the one you saw? I saw a deer the was Cayenne Brown.

Acorn Brown

Cayenne Brown

Hickory Brown

Gingerbread Brown

Tawny Brown

The color Grey is a perfect neutral color because it is created with the colors black and white. Grey is often used as a background color for designers or photographers.

The color Grey is known as one of the least popular colors.

There are alot of birds, fish and land animals that are the color Grey because Grey makes a natural camouflage and allows the animals to blend into their surroundings.

The color Grey is usually associated with older people and Grey hair.
Does your grandma or grandpa have Grey hair?

This is my White page.
I like to try to pop the
balloons with my paw
when mom blows them
up. Have you ever
popped a balloon?

This White teddy bear is
one of my favorite toys.
Do you have a teddy bear?

White Teddy Bear

White flower

Balloons

Golf Ball

White flower
petals

The color White is a safe and happy color.

White is a positive color and stands for innocence, light, heaven, safety, cleanliness, protection, softness and perfection.

In the Western countries, White is the traditional color worn by brides to stand for innocence. In Eastern countries, the people wear White when someone dies and to funerals.

White is the color of snow and is often thought about as being a cool and a very simple color.

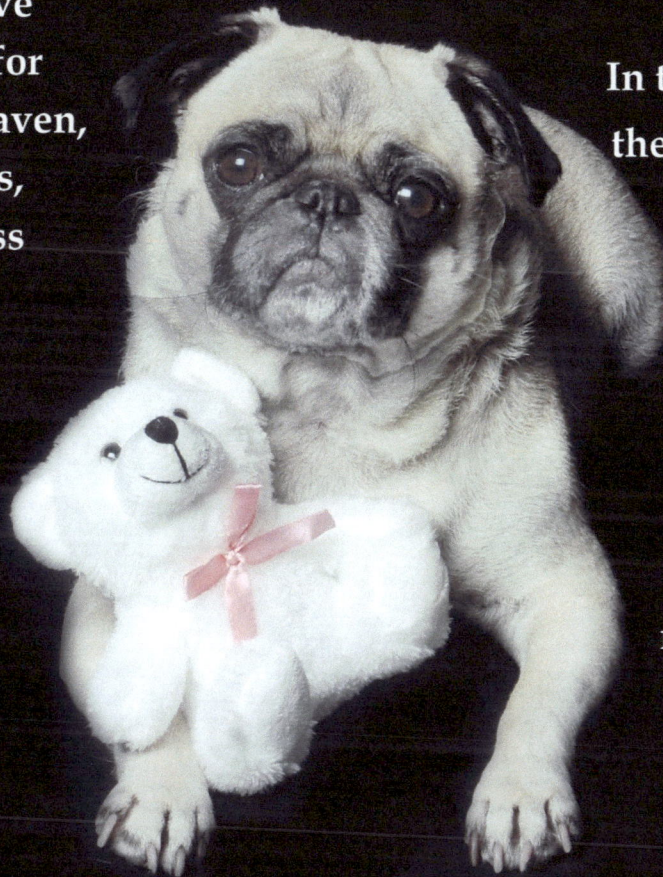

In other cultures, White is the color of royalty or of religious figures (ex: angels).

Red + Yellow makes Orange

Trace my
footsteps
with your
finger
and see
what happens
when you
mix colors.

Blue + Yellow makes Green

Blue + Red makes
Purple

ABOUT MOLLY PAGE

Miss Molly Mia is a five year old pug who lives in Kansas with her people. She loves to take walks, eat treats, get belly rubs, take a bath, take naps and go bye bye. This is Molly's fifth book in a 10-book series. We hope that you enjoy reading and learning from these books as much as Molly enjoyed creating them for you. Molly's next book will be a shape book.

Thanks for reading my color book!! My books are available on Amazon or on the FB page: Author Candy Johansen.